THE 7 HABITS OF ZEN LEADERSHIP

What Successful Leaders Did
When The World Stopped
Going to Work

TIM SALAU

Mr. Future of Work (FoW)

Dedication

"To the leaders who dare to lead differently."

Acknowledgments

This book is dedicated to my loving family, my amazing friends, Blessing Adogame, & our Guide community.

Table of Contents

PART I
The Foundations of Zen Leadership

Chapter 1

PART II
The 7 Habits of Zen Leadership

Chapter 2

Chapter 3

Chapter 4

Chapter 5

Chapter 6

The Zen Leadership Imperative

Why the World Needs a New Kind of Leader

In March 2020, the world stopped. Offices emptied. Schools closed. Streets fell silent. Leaders faced a question they'd never asked before: *What does work mean when the office vanishes?*

The pandemic didn't just disrupt workflows—it shattered illusions. Hierarchies crumbled under Zoom fatigue. Surveillance tools meant to "track productivity" bred resentment. Burnout spiked as employees juggled childcare, grief, and endless video calls. The old playbook—rigid structures, profit-over-people mandates, and command-and-control tactics—failed. But amid the chaos, a new breed of leader emerged.

These leaders didn't cling to the past. They didn't panic. They *pivoted*—not just tactically, but philosophically. Microsoft redefined productivity as outcomes, not hours logged. Patagonia doubled down on climate activism while keeping employees whole. Chobani turned factories into community lifelines. Spotify's squads innovated faster than ever. What united them? A commitment to **Zen Leadership**: a blend of purpose, humanity, and agility that prioritizes *people* over process and *legacy* over short-term wins.

Zen Leadership isn't about meditation or mindfulness (though presence matters). It's about rejecting the myth that leaders must choose between results and compassion. It's recognizing that in a world of climate crises, AI disruption, and fractured trust, the old models of leadership aren't just outdated—they're dangerous.

This book is your guide to leading differently. Through seven habits—forged in the fires of the pandemic and tested by today's relentless challenges—you'll learn how to:

- **Anchor teams in purpose** when uncertainty swirls.

- **Build trust** by replacing surveillance with radical empathy.

- **Turn crisis into innovation** with decentralized, agile teams.

- **Lead boldly** without sacrificing humanity.

The stories here aren't theory. They're battle-tested blueprints from leaders who thrived when the world stopped. Their lessons are urgent, their tools practical, and their vision clear: *The future of work isn't about returning to "normal." It's about building something better.*

If you're ready to lead in a world that demands more—more courage, more creativity, more care—this book is your manifesto. Let's begin.

PART I

The Foundations of Zen Leadership

The Future of Work is NOW

The Crisis & The Opportunity

In March 2020, the world stopped. Offices emptied, commutes vanished, and leaders faced a question they'd never asked before: *What does work look like when the office is gone?* For Microsoft, the answer wasn't just about tools or technology—it was about reimagining work itself.

Satya Nadella, Microsoft's CEO, didn't panic. Instead, he saw an opportunity to live out the company's mission: *"Empower every person and organization on the planet to achieve more."* But this wasn't just a slogan. It was a call to action. Over the next year, Microsoft didn't just adapt to remote work—it redefined it.

The Story of Microsoft's Pivot
The Early Days: Chaos and Clarity

When the pandemic hit, Microsoft's leadership team faced a whirlwind of decisions. Offices were closing, employees were scrambling to set up home offices, and customers were demanding solutions. But amid the chaos, Nadella kept asking one question: *"How do we stay true to our mission?"*

The answer came in the form of Teams, Microsoft's collaboration platform. Overnight, Teams became the lifeline for millions of workers. But Microsoft didn't stop there. They saw this moment as a chance to rethink work itself—not just for their employees, but for the world.

The Turning Point: Flexibility as a Core Value

In July 2020, Microsoft released its *Hybrid Work Playbook*, a guide for leaders navigating the new normal. The message was clear: *"Work is an activity, not a place."* Employees were given the freedom to choose where and when they worked.

But this wasn't just about flexibility—it was about trust. Microsoft rejected the idea of tracking employees' every move. Instead, they focused on outcomes. Managers were trained to measure results, not hours.

The Innovation: "Together Mode"

One of Microsoft's most talked-about innovations was "Together Mode" on Teams. This feature used AI to place video participants in shared virtual spaces, like coffee shops or auditoriums. The goal? To combat

"Zoom fatigue" and make virtual meetings feel more human.

The response was overwhelming. Teams' daily active users skyrocketed from 32 million in 2019 to 145 million in 2021. But the real win wasn't the numbers—it was the culture shift. Employees felt empowered, not policed.

The Human Side: Prioritizing Well-Being

Microsoft didn't just focus on productivity—they prioritized people. Early in the pandemic, Nadella noticed a troubling trend: burnout was on the rise. Employees were working longer hours, juggling childcare, and struggling to disconnect.

So Microsoft took action. They introduced "Wellness Days"—extra paid days off for mental health. They partnered with apps like Headspace to offer free meditation resources. And they encouraged leaders to model vulnerability.

Nadella led by example. In his memoir, *Hit Refresh*, he wrote about his own struggles with burnout. *"I had to learn to pace myself,"* he shared. *"Empathy starts with self-awareness."*

This focus on well-being paid off. Employee satisfaction scores soared, and attrition dropped to a five-year low.

The Results: A New Way of Working

By the end of 2020, Microsoft's revenue had grown 17%, hitting $143 billion. But the real success wasn't in the numbers—it was in the culture. Employees felt supported, customers felt empowered, and the world took notice.

Actionable Takeaways for Leaders

1. Redefine Your "Office"

   The pandemic proved that work isn't a place—it's a mindset. To thrive in the new world of work, leaders need to rethink their policies.

   - **Conduct a Purpose Audit:** Ask, *"Do our office policies align with our mission?"* For example, a healthcare company realized mandatory office days conflicted with its goal to *"put patients first."* They shifted to hybrid schedules, letting clinicians spend more time in communities.

   - **Build a Hybrid Work Policy:** Start with core hours (e.g., 10 AM–2 PM for meetings) and invest in tools like Loom for video updates.

   - **Train Managers:** Focus on outcome-based goals, not micromanagement.

2. Normalize Humanity

The pandemic reminded us that employees are people, not machines. To build trust, leaders need to prioritize well-being.

- **Redesign 1:1 Meetings:** Replace "What's your progress?" with "How are you really?"

- **Implement "Virtual Commute" Rituals:** Borrow Microsoft's Teams feature: A 5-minute wind-down reminder with calming visuals and prompts like *"What's one win from today?"*

- **Model Vulnerability:** Share your own struggles with burnout.

3. Eliminate "Presenteeism"

The old 9-to-5 office model is dead. To thrive, leaders need to focus on results, not face time.

- **No-Meeting Fridays:** A SaaS company reduced meeting hours by 40% and saw a 15% rise in code deployment speed.

- **Async Updates:** Use tools like Notion for project tracking and Loom for video updates.

- **Deep Work Sprints:** Use the *Pomodoro Technique* (25 minutes focused work, 5-minute break) with a mindfulness bell app.

Pitfalls to Avoid

1. Surveillance Over Trust

    Some companies responded to remote work by installing keystroke-tracking software. The result? A 34% drop in morale and a class-action lawsuit.

    - **Fix:** Publish a "Trust Charter" outlining how performance will be measured (e.g., outcomes, not screen time).

2. Ignoring Equity

    Mandating office returns can disadvantage caregivers and disabled employees.

    - **Fix:** Create a "Flexibility Task Force" to audit policies for inclusivity.

Your "Future-Proof" Workshop

Step 1: Team Retrospective

Ask your team: "What's one outdated rule we should abandon?"

- Example Answers:

    - "Mandatory 8 AM meetings."

    - "Requiring approval for remote work."

Step 2: Zen Visualization Exercise

Guide your team through a meditation: "Close your eyes. Imagine your ideal workplace. What does it smell like? How do colleagues interact? Write down 3 words that describe this culture."

Step 3: Build a 90-Day Plan

- Month 1: Pilot hybrid meetings (e.g., 3 days remote, 2 days in-office).

- Month 2: Launch wellness initiatives (e.g., meditation stipends).

- Month 3: Audit tools (e.g., replace Slack with Teams if collaboration improves).

Chapter Summary

The pandemic proved that the future of work isn't a distant concept—it's here. Leaders like Microsoft thrived by:

1. Anchoring decisions in their mission.

2. Embracing flexibility and trust.

3. Prioritizing well-being over hustle.

Your next step isn't to "return to normal" but to **build better**. Let go of relics like presenteeism, and create a culture where flexibility and humanity drive results.

Think about it: What's one policy or practice in your organization that conflicts with your core mission? How could you realign it to better serve your purpose?

Next Chapter Preview:

Chapter 2: Lead with Purpose ('Why') explores how Patagonia's mission to *"save our home planet"* fueled bold climate action—and how to craft a *Why* that inspires your team.

PART II

The 7 Habits of Zen Leadership

Lead with Purpose ('Why')

The Crisis & The Opportunity

In 1973, Yvon Chouinard, a climber and blacksmith, founded Patagonia with a simple mission: "Build the best product, cause no unnecessary harm, use business to inspire and implement solutions to the environmental crisis." Decades later, this mission isn't just a tagline—it's the heartbeat of the company.

When the pandemic hit, Patagonia didn't just survive—it thrived. Why? Because its *Why*—its purpose—wasn't just about selling outdoor gear. It was about saving the planet. This chapter explores how Patagonia's unwavering commitment to its mission fueled bold action during the pandemic—and how you can lead with purpose in times of crisis.

The Story of Patagonia's Purpose
The Early Days: A Climber's Ethos

Yvon Chouinard didn't set out to build a billion-dollar company. He just wanted to make better climbing gear.

But as he scaled mountains, he noticed something troubling: the environment was deteriorating.

In the 1980s, Patagonia made a bold decision: it would donate 1% of its sales to environmental causes. This wasn't a marketing ploy—it was a reflection of Chouinard's values. *"If we're not part of the solution,"* he said, *"we're part of the problem."*

The Turning Point: "Don't Buy This Jacket"

In 2011, Patagonia ran a full-page ad in *The New York Times* with a shocking headline: *"Don't Buy This Jacket."* The ad urged consumers to think twice before purchasing, emphasizing the environmental cost of overconsumption.

The campaign was risky, but it worked. Sales soared, and Patagonia's reputation as a purpose-driven brand was cemented.

The Pandemic: Staying True to the Mission

When COVID-19 forced stores to close, Patagonia didn't panic. Instead, it doubled down on its mission. The company shifted its focus to online sales and used its platform to advocate for environmental justice.

In 2020, Patagonia launched *Action Works*, a digital hub connecting customers with local environmental organizations. The message was clear: *"We're not just selling products—we're building a movement."*

The Human Side: Empowering Employees

Patagonia's purpose isn't just external—it's internal. Employees are encouraged to live out the company's values, both at work and at home.

Wellness and Activism

During the pandemic, Patagonia introduced *"Environmental Internships,"* allowing employees to take paid time off to work with environmental nonprofits. The program wasn't just about giving back—it was about empowering employees to live out the company's mission.

Leadership by Example

Rose Marcario, Patagonia's CEO from 2014 to 2020, was a vocal advocate for environmental and social justice. Under her leadership, Patagonia became the first California company to become a certified B Corporation, meeting rigorous standards for social and environmental performance.

Marcario's mantra was simple: *"We're in business to save our home planet."* This clarity of purpose inspired employees, customers, and even competitors.

The Results: A Movement, Not Just a Brand

By staying true to its mission, Patagonia didn't just survive the pandemic—it thrived. In 2020, the company's revenue grew by 17%, and its customer loyalty reached an all-time high.

But the real success wasn't in the numbers—it was in the impact. Patagonia's advocacy helped pass landmark environmental legislation, and its *Action Works* platform connected thousands of people with local causes.

Actionable Takeaways for Leaders

1. Define Your 'Why'

   Your purpose isn't just a mission statement—it's your North Star. To define your *Why*, ask:

   - "What problem are we solving?"

   - "What legacy do we want to leave?"

Example: A tech company realized its *Why* wasn't just about building software—it was about *"empowering small businesses to thrive."* This clarity inspired a new product line focused on affordable tools for entrepreneurs.

2. Align Actions with Values

   Purpose without action is just words. To live out your *Why*, align every decision—big and small—with your mission.

- **Product Development:** Ask, "Does this align with our values?"

- **Marketing:** Use your platform to advocate for your cause.

- **Community Engagement:** Partner with organizations that share your mission.

Example: A fashion brand committed to sustainability launched a *"Repair, Don't Replace"* program, offering free repairs for damaged clothing.

3. Empower Employees to Live the Mission

   Your employees are your greatest ambassadors. To inspire them, give them opportunities to live out your *Why*.

- **Volunteer Programs:** Offer paid time off for community service.

- **Internal Advocacy:** Create employee-led committees to drive social and environmental initiatives.

- **Leadership Training:** Teach managers to lead with purpose, not just profits.

Example: A healthcare company introduced *"Wellness Champions,"* employees trained to promote mental health and well-being in the workplace.

Pitfalls to Avoid

1. Purpose Washing

    Some companies use purpose as a marketing tool without backing it up with action. This can lead to backlash and loss of trust.

    *   **Fix:** Ensure your actions match your words. Be transparent about your progress and challenges.

2. Ignoring Stakeholders

    Purpose-driven leadership isn't just about customers—it's about employees, communities, and the planet.

    *   **Fix:** Engage all stakeholders in your mission. Conduct regular surveys to gather feedback and ideas.

3. Short-Term Thinking

    Purpose isn't a quick fix—it's a long-term commitment.

    *   **Fix:** Set measurable goals and track progress over time. Celebrate small wins to keep momentum alive.

Your "Purpose-Driven Leadership" Workshop

Step 1: Define Your 'Why'

- Gather your team and ask: "What problem are we solving? What legacy do we want to leave?"

- Use the *Golden Circle* framework: Start with *Why*, then define *How* and *What*.

Step 2: Align Actions with Values

- Conduct a *Purpose Audit*: Review your products, policies, and partnerships. Do they align with your mission?

- Identify one area for improvement and create a 90-day action plan.

Step 3: Empower Employees

- Launch a *Purpose Ambassador Program*: Train employees to champion your mission.

- Host a *Purpose Day*: Dedicate a day to community service or advocacy.

Chapter Summary

Patagonia's story proves that purpose isn't just a nice-to-have—it's a must-have. By staying true to its mission, the company not only survived the pandemic but emerged stronger, more resilient, and more impactful.

Your next step is to define your *Why* and align every decision with your mission. When you lead with purpose, you don't just build a business—you build a movement.

Think about it: If you had to explain your team's "Why" in one sentence, what would it be? Where are you currently sacrificing purpose for short-term gains?

Next Chapter Preview:

Chapter 3: Lead with Authenticity explores how Netflix's culture of radical transparency helped it navigate the streaming wars—and how you can build trust through authenticity.

Lead with Authenticity

The Crisis & The Opportunity

In 2011, Netflix faced a defining moment. CEO Reed Hastings announced a controversial decision: splitting the company into two separate entities—Netflix for streaming and Qwikster for DVD rentals. Customers revolted. The stock plummeted 77% in four months. Employees were confused, and critics declared Netflix dead.

But Hastings didn't backtrack. Instead, he doubled down on a core tenet of Netflix's culture: *radical transparency*. He admitted the mistake, apologized publicly, and scrapped Qwikster. Then, he did something even bolder—he published a 124-page slide deck detailing Netflix's culture of "Freedom and Responsibility." The document went viral, attracting millions of views and top talent.

Netflix didn't just recover—it became a $200 billion streaming giant. This chapter explores how Netflix's commitment to authenticity—even in failure—built trust, fueled innovation, and redefined leadership.

The Story of Netflix's Authenticity

The Early Days: No Rules, Just Principles

When Reed Hastings co-founded Netflix in 1997, he wanted to build a company where employees acted like "stakesholders, not employees." The mantra? *"Freedom and Responsibility."*

In practice, this meant:

- No vacation policies (take as much as you need).

- No expense approvals (spend the company's money like it's your own).

- Radical candor in feedback (even CEOs get blunt critiques).

The Turning Point: The Culture Deck

In 2009, Netflix's culture document leaked online. Instead of panicking, Hastings leaned in. He revised and published it publicly in 2011. The deck outlined principles like:

- "Only hire, reward, and tolerate fully formed adults."

- *"Sunshining"*: Publicly admitting mistakes to build trust.

The transparency shocked corporate America. But it worked. Top talent flocked to Netflix, drawn by its rejection of bureaucracy and embrace of autonomy.

The Pandemic Test: Authenticity Under Pressure

When COVID-19 hit, Netflix faced a new challenge: keeping creativity alive in a remote world. Instead of surveilling employees, Netflix doubled down on trust.

- **No Productivity Tracking:** Employees set their own hours.

- **"Context, Not Control":** Leaders shared strategic goals but let teams decide *how* to achieve them.

- **Radical Feedback:** Virtual "360 reviews" became even more candid.

The result? Subscriptions surged by 37 million in 2020, and hits like *The Queen's Gambit* and *Bridgerton* dominated pop culture.

The Human Side: Building Trust Through Candor

Netflix's culture isn't for everyone. But for those who thrive, it's transformative.

The Keeper Test

Managers regularly ask: *"If this person quit tomorrow, would I fight to keep them?"* If the answer is no, the employee is let go—with generous severance. This practice ensures teams are filled with high performers who align with Netflix's values.

Sunshining Failures

After the Qwikster debacle, Hastings didn't hide. He wrote a blog post titled *"I Messed Up,"* detailing lessons learned. This vulnerability became a cultural norm. Teams now start meetings by sharing recent mistakes.

Employee Empowerment

Netflix's famous "No Vacation Policy" isn't about unlimited days off—it's about treating adults like adults. Employees are trusted to balance work and life without micromanagement.

The Results: Trust Fuels Innovation

By 2023, Netflix had 238 million subscribers and 70+ Emmy wins. But its real legacy is its culture:

- **Top Talent Retention:** Voluntary attrition is 3-4%, far below the tech industry average (13%).

- **Speed of Innovation:** Netflix releases a new original title *every week*, a pace competitors can't match.

- **Customer Loyalty:** 93% of subscribers say they'll stick with Netflix despite price hikes.

Actionable Takeaways for Leaders

1. Define Your Non-Negotiables

Authenticity starts with clarity. Identify 3-4 cultural pillars that define your organization.

- **Example:** A fintech startup adopted Netflix's "Freedom and Responsibility" model, replacing strict deadlines with *"Impact Goals."* Productivity rose 22%.

- Template:
    - *Pillar 1:* Radical Candor (e.g., "Feedback is a gift").
    - *Pillar 2:* Ownership (e.g., "Act like a CEO").
    - *Pillar 3:* No BS (e.g., "Say what you mean").

2. Practice Radical Transparency

Build trust by over-communicating—even when it's uncomfortable.

- **Sunshining Ritual:** Start leadership meetings with a "Failure of the Week" share.

- **Open-Book Management:** Share financials, strategy, and board updates with all employees.

- **Public Apologies:** When you screw up, admit it openly.

3. Empower, Don't Control

Trust your team to make decisions without hand-holding.

- **Abolish Micromanagement:**

  Eliminate approval layers for small budgets (e.g., under $10k).

- **Flexible Work:** Let employees choose *where* and *when* they work. Measure outcomes, not hours.

- **Autonomous Teams:** Give teams ownership of projects from ideation to execution.

Pitfalls to Avoid

1. Toxic Transparency

Radical candor can backfire if it becomes brutal honesty.

- **Fix:** Train teams to deliver feedback with empathy. Use the *SBI Model* (Situation-Behavior-Impact).

2. Inconsistent Actions

Employees spot hypocrisy instantly. If your culture deck says "No Rules" but you enforce strict PTO policies, trust erodes.

- **Fix:** Audit policies quarterly. Ask, "Does this align with our cultural pillars?"

3. Hiring Misalignment

Not everyone thrives in an autonomous culture.

- **Fix:** Use the Keeper Test in interviews: "Would I fight to hire this person again?"

Your "Authentic Leadership" Workshop

Step 1: Define Your Cultural Pillars

- Gather your team and ask: "What 3-4 values define us at our best?"

- Example: A healthcare company chose *Candor, Compassion, Curiosity.*

Step 2: Conduct a Transparency Audit

- Review:

    - How openly do leaders share bad news?

    - Do employees feel safe admitting mistakes?

- Identify one area to improve (e.g., launch a "Failure Forum").

Step 3: Empower Your Team

- Pilot a "No Approval Zone": Let teams make decisions under a set budget without oversight.

- Host a "Feedback Fest": Role-play giving and receiving candid feedback.

Chapter Summary

Netflix's journey proves that authenticity isn't about being perfect—it's about being real. By embracing radical transparency, empowering employees, and owning mistakes, Netflix built a culture where trust drives innovation.

Your move: Tear up the rulebook, define your non-negotiables, and lead with unapologetic authenticity.

Think about it: When was the last time you shared a personal failure or vulnerability with your team? What's stopping you from doing it more often?

Next Chapter Preview:

Chapter 4: Lead with Adaptability dives into Spotify's "Squad Model" and how agile teams can pivot faster than competitors in times of chaos.

Lead with Adaptability

The Crisis & The Opportunity

In 2020, as the world grappled with the COVID-19 pandemic, Spotify faced a unique challenge. With millions of people suddenly working from home, commuting less, and spending more time indoors, the demand for entertainment skyrocketed. But so did the competition. Streaming platforms like Netflix, YouTube, and Apple Music were all vying for attention in an increasingly crowded market.

Spotify's response? Double down on adaptability. The company's agile "Squad Model," which had been a cornerstone of its culture for years, allowed it to pivot faster than its competitors. While other companies struggled to adjust, Spotify thrived, adding millions of new users and launching innovative features like **Spotify Wrapped** and **Group Sessions**. This chapter explores how Spotify's commitment to adaptability helped it navigate chaos—and how you can lead with agility in times of uncertainty.

The Story of Spotify's Adaptability
The Early Days: The Birth of the Squad Model

When Spotify was founded in 2006, its mission was simple: to give people access to the world's music. But as the company grew, so did its complexity. By 2012, Spotify had hundreds of employees across multiple countries, and traditional hierarchical structures were slowing it down. That's when the company introduced the **Squad Model**, a radical new way of organizing teams.

The Squad Model is based on the principles of **agile development**, a methodology originally used in software engineering. At Spotify, squads are small, cross-functional teams that operate like mini-startups. Each squad has a clear mission, such as improving the user experience or developing new algorithms for personalized playlists. Squads are autonomous, meaning they have the freedom to decide how to achieve their goals without waiting for approval from higher-ups.

The Turning Point: Scaling Agility

As Spotify grew, so did the number of squads. By 2014, the company had over 100 squads working on everything from music recommendations to ad sales. To manage this complexity, Spotify introduced **tribes**, **chapters**, and **guilds**—structures designed to maintain alignment while preserving autonomy.

- **Tribes**: Groups of squads working on related projects (e.g., the "Music Tribe").

- **Chapters**: Functional groups within a tribe (e.g., backend engineers).

- **Guilds**: Cross-tribe communities of interest (e.g., data science enthusiasts).

This structure allowed Spotify to scale its agility without sacrificing innovation. Squads could move fast, experiment, and iterate, while tribes and guilds ensured that everyone stayed aligned with the company's overall mission.

The Pandemic Test: Adapting to a New Normal

When COVID-19 hit, Spotify's adaptability was put to the test. With people stuck at home, the company saw a surge in demand for podcasts, playlists, and other audio content. But the pandemic also brought new challenges, such as disrupted supply chains and shifting consumer behavior.

Spotify's response was swift. The company accelerated the rollout of new features, such as **Group Sessions**, which allowed users to listen to music together in real-time, even when physically apart. It also doubled down on podcasts, signing exclusive deals with high-profile creators like Joe Rogan and Michelle Obama. By the end of 2020, Spotify had added over 30 million new users, bringing its total to over 345 million.

The Human Side: Empowering Teams to Adapt

At the heart of Spotify's adaptability is its culture of trust and empowerment. Employees are encouraged to take risks, experiment, and learn from failure. This culture is supported by several key practices:

1. Psychological Safety

    Spotify's squads operate in an environment where it's safe to take risks and make mistakes. Leaders encourage open dialogue and constructive feedback, ensuring that everyone feels heard and valued.

2. Continuous Learning

    Spotify invests heavily in employee development. Squads regularly hold retrospectives to reflect on what's working and what's not. These sessions are not about assigning blame but about learning and improving.

3. Decentralized Decision-Making

   By giving squads the autonomy to make decisions,
   Spotify ensures that decisions are made quickly and
   close to the problem. This reduces bottlenecks and
   allows the company to respond to changes in real-
   time.

The Results: Agility Fuels Growth

By 2023, Spotify had become the world's largest audio
streaming platform, with over 500 million users and 200
million subscribers. But its real success lies in its ability
to adapt. Whether it's launching new features, entering
new markets, or responding to global crises, Spotify's
agility has allowed it to stay ahead of the competition.

Actionable Takeaways for Leaders

1. Adopt Agile Principles

   Agility starts with structure. Consider implementing
   a version of Spotify's Squad Model in your
   organization.

   - **Start Small:** Pilot a cross-functional team with
     a clear mission and autonomy.

   - **Scale Gradually:** As the team succeeds, expand
     the model to other parts of the organization.

- **Measure Outcomes:** Focus on results, not processes.

2. Foster Psychological Safety

   Adaptability requires trust. Create an environment where employees feel safe to take risks and voice their opinions.

   - **Encourage Open Dialogue:** Hold regular team retrospectives to discuss what's working and what's not.

   - **Normalize Failure:** Celebrate lessons learned from mistakes, not just successes.

   - **Lead by Example:** Model vulnerability by sharing your own failures and learnings.

3. Decentralize Decision-Making

   Speed is critical in times of uncertainty. Empower teams to make decisions without waiting for approval.

   - **Clarify Boundaries:** Define the scope of autonomy for each team.

   - **Provide Context:** Share strategic goals and priorities to ensure alignment.

- **Trust Your People:** Resist the urge to micromanage.

Pitfalls to Avoid

1. Overcomplicating Agility

   Agility is about simplicity, not bureaucracy. Avoid creating too many layers or processes.

   - **Fix:** Regularly audit your structures to ensure they're enabling, not hindering, agility.

2. Ignoring Alignment

   Autonomy without alignment leads to chaos. Ensure that teams are working toward shared goals.

   - **Fix:** Use tools like OKRs (Objectives and Key Results) to keep everyone aligned.

3. Neglecting Culture

   Agility requires a culture of trust and empowerment. Without it, even the best structures will fail.

   - **Fix:** Invest in cultural initiatives that promote psychological safety and continuous learning.

Your "Adaptability Leadership" Workshop

Step 1: Pilot a Squad

- Identify a small, cross-functional team and give them a clear mission.

- Provide autonomy and resources, then step back and let them work.

Step 2: Conduct a Retrospective

- Gather your team and ask: "What's one thing we could do to become more agile?"

- Use the feedback to identify areas for improvement.

Step 3: Define Your Agile Principles

- Work with your team to define 3–4 principles that will guide your approach to agility.

- Example: "Fail fast, learn faster," "Decisions are made closest to the problem," "Trust over control."

Chapter Summary

Spotify's story proves that adaptability isn't just a buzzword—it's a survival skill. By embracing agile principles, fostering psychological safety, and decentralizing decision-making, Spotify thrived in the face of uncertainty. Your next step is to lead with adaptability: tear down silos, empower your teams, and create a culture where agility drives innovation.

Think about it: What's one outdated process or rule slowing your team down? How could you test a bolder, more agile approach this month?

Next Chapter Preview:

Chapter 5: Lead with Boldness explores how HEB's audacious adaptability and risk-taking culture helped it revolutionize the grocery industry—and how you can lead with boldness in your own organization.

Lead with Boldness

The Crisis & The Opportunity

In 2020, as the COVID-19 pandemic swept across the globe, grocery stores became ground zero for the crisis. Panic buying, supply chain disruptions, and workforce shortages created unprecedented challenges for retailers. National chains like Walmart and Kroger struggled to keep shelves stocked and customers safe. But in Texas, one grocery chain stood out for its bold, decisive actions: **HEB**.

While other retailers scrambled to react, HEB was already steps ahead. The company had a pandemic response plan in place long before COVID-19 hit, thanks to its experience dealing with hurricanes and other emergencies in Texas. When the pandemic struck, HEB swiftly implemented safety measures, secured supply chains, and even launched innovative services like curbside pickup and home delivery at scale. By the end of 2020, HEB had not only survived the crisis but emerged stronger, with record sales and even deeper customer loyalty.

HEB's success is a testament to the power of bold leadership—the willingness to take risks, act decisively, and prioritize long-term impact over short-term gains. This chapter explores how HEB's boldness has made it a dominant force in the Texas grocery market—and how you can lead with boldness to drive innovation and resilience in your own organization.

The Story of HEB's Boldness

The Early Days: A Family-Owned Vision

HEB's story begins in 1905, when Florence Butt opened a small grocery store in Kerrville, Texas. From the beginning, the company was guided by a simple mission: to provide the best value and service to its customers. Over the decades, HEB grew from a single store to a regional powerhouse, but it never lost sight of its roots. Today, HEB is still privately owned and operated by the Butt family, with over 400 stores across Texas and Mexico.

What sets HEB apart is its bold commitment to innovation and community. While other grocery chains focus on cutting costs and maximizing profits, HEB invests heavily in its people, products, and communities. This bold approach has allowed HEB to dominate the Texas market, even as national competitors like Walmart and Kroger struggle to gain a foothold.

The Turning Point: Hurricane Harvey and Disaster Preparedness

HEB's boldness was put to the test in 2017, when Hurricane Harvey devastated Texas. The storm caused widespread flooding, displacing thousands of people and disrupting supply chains. But HEB was ready. The company had a disaster response plan in place, which included pre-positioning supplies, mobilizing its fleet of mobile kitchens, and deploying its emergency response team to affected areas.

During the crisis, HEB provided free meals, water, and supplies to first responders and affected communities. The company also kept its stores open, often at a loss, to ensure that people had access to food and essentials. HEB's bold response to Hurricane Harvey earned it widespread praise and cemented its reputation as a company that truly cares about its customers.

The Innovation: Redefining the Grocery Experience

HEB's boldness isn't limited to crisis response. The company has consistently redefined the grocery experience through innovation and customer-centric strategies:

1. Private Label Excellence

   HEB's private label brands, such as **HEB Organics** and **Hill Country Fare**, are known for their high quality and affordability. The company invests heavily in product development, often working directly with local farmers and producers to create unique offerings. This bold focus on private label has allowed HEB to differentiate itself from competitors and build customer loyalty.

2. Curbside Pickup and Home Delivery

   Long before the pandemic, HEB was a pioneer in online grocery shopping. The company launched its curbside pickup service in 2015 and quickly expanded it to all of its stores. During the pandemic, HEB scaled up its home delivery service, partnering with third-party providers like Instacart to meet surging demand. This bold investment in e-commerce paid off, with online sales growing by over 200% in 2020.

3. Community Engagement

   HEB's boldest move is its deep commitment to the communities it serves. The company donates 5% of its pre-tax profits to charitable causes, including education, hunger relief, and disaster recovery. HEB also supports local schools, hospitals, and nonprofits through its **HEB Community Investment Program**. This bold focus on community has earned HEB unparalleled customer loyalty and goodwill.

The Pandemic Test: Boldness in Action

When COVID-19 hit, HEB's boldness was once again on full display. The company quickly implemented safety measures, such as plexiglass barriers, social distancing markers, and mandatory masks for employees. It also launched a **"Texans Helping Texans"** campaign, providing free meals to healthcare workers and donating millions of dollars to food banks.

But HEB's boldest move during the pandemic was its decision to prioritize people over profits. The company invested $50 million in employee bonuses and wage increases, recognizing the critical role its frontline workers played in keeping stores open and customers fed. HEB also waived fees for curbside pickup and home delivery, even as demand surged and costs rose.

By the end of 2020, HEB's boldness had paid off. The company reported record sales and customer satisfaction, with many Texans declaring their loyalty to HEB for life.

The Human Side: Cultivating a Culture of Boldness

At the heart of HEB's boldness is its culture of empowerment, innovation, and community. Employees are encouraged to think big, take risks, and put customers first. This culture is supported by several key practices:

1. Employee-Centric Leadership

   HEB's leaders, including CEO Charles Butt, are deeply committed to their employees. The company offers competitive wages, benefits, and opportunities for advancement, creating a loyal and motivated workforce. During the pandemic, HEB's decision to invest in employee bonuses and wage increases was a bold statement of its commitment to its people.

2. Decentralized Decision-Making

   HEB empowers its store managers and employees to make decisions that benefit their local communities. This decentralized approach allows HEB to respond quickly to local needs and preferences, giving it a competitive edge over national chains.

3. Continuous Innovation

   HEB's culture of innovation is driven by its willingness to experiment and take risks. The company regularly tests new products, services, and technologies, often rolling them out in select stores before expanding to others. This bold approach to innovation keeps HEB ahead of the curve.

4. Community First

   HEB's boldest cultural pillar is its commitment to community. Employees are encouraged to volunteer, donate, and support local causes, creating a sense of purpose and pride in their work. This community-first mindset has earned HEB the trust and loyalty of its customers.

The Results: Boldness Fuels Dominance

By 2023, HEB had solidified its position as the dominant grocery chain in Texas, with a market share of over 50% in many regions. The company's boldness had paid off in several key ways:

- **Customer Loyalty:** HEB's Net Promoter Score (NPS) is consistently among the highest in the industry, reflecting its deep connection with customers.

- **Employee Satisfaction:** HEB's employee turnover rate is significantly lower than the industry average, thanks to its employee-centric culture.

- **Community Impact:** HEB's charitable contributions and community programs have made it a beloved institution in Texas.

But HEB's real legacy lies in its ability to inspire others. The company's boldness has shown that a regional brand can not only compete with national giants but also set new standards for innovation, customer service, and community engagement.

Actionable Takeaways for Leaders

1. Define Your Bold Mission

   Boldness starts with a clear, inspiring mission that guides your decisions and actions.

   - **Ask:** "What's the biggest impact we can make in our community or industry?"

   - **Example:** HEB's mission to "provide the best value and service to our customers" is both bold and customer-centric.

   - **Template:** "Our mission is to [solve a major problem] by [specific outcome]."

2. Invest in Your People

   Bold leaders prioritize their employees, recognizing that they are the key to long-term success.

   - **Offer Competitive Benefits:** Provide wages, benefits, and opportunities that attract and retain top talent.

   - **Empower Employees:** Give employees the autonomy and resources they need to make decisions and take risks.

   - **Recognize Contributions:** Celebrate employee achievements and contributions, especially during challenging times.

3. Embrace Innovation

   Boldness requires a willingness to experiment and take risks.

   - **Test New Ideas:** Pilot new products, services, and technologies in select markets before scaling up

   - **Learn from Failure:** Create a culture where failure is seen as a learning opportunity, not a setback.

- **Stay Ahead of Trends:** Continuously monitor industry trends and customer preferences to stay ahead of the competition.

4. Prioritize Community

   Bold leaders understand the importance of giving back to their communities.

   - **Support Local Causes:** Invest in charitable initiatives that align with your mission and values.

   - **Engage Employees:** Encourage employees to volunteer and participate in community programs.

   - **Build Trust:** Demonstrate your commitment to the community through consistent actions and transparency.

Pitfalls to Avoid

1. Overextending Resources

   Boldness requires resources, but overextending can lead to burnout and failure.

   - **Fix:** Prioritize initiatives and allocate resources strategically.

2. Ignoring Feedback

   Bold leaders must be open to feedback and willing to adjust their approach.

   - **Fix:** Create channels for employees and customers to share feedback and ideas.

3. Losing Focus

   Boldness is about staying focused on your mission, even in the face of distractions.

   - **Fix:** Regularly revisit your mission and values to ensure alignment with your actions.

Your "Bold Leadership" Workshop

Step 1: Define Your Bold Mission

   - Gather your team and ask: "What's the biggest impact we can make in our community or industry?"

   - Use the **Golden Circle** framework: Start with *Why*, then define *How* and *What*.

Step 2: Identify Bold Opportunities

   - Brainstorm bold ideas that align with your mission.

- Use the **Moonshot Thinking** framework: "What would we do if we had unlimited resources?"

Step 3: Create a Bold Action Plan

- Identify 2–3 bold initiatives to pursue in the next 90 days.

- Assign ownership and resources to each initiative.

- Set milestones to track progress and celebrate successes.

Chapter Summary

HEB's story proves that boldness is not just a leadership trait—it's a mindset. By defining a bold mission, investing in people, embracing innovation, and prioritizing community, HEB has become a dominant force in the Texas grocery market and a model for others to follow. Your next step is to lead with boldness: take risks, act decisively, and create a culture where boldness drives innovation and resilience.

Think about it: What's a risk you've avoided taking because it feels too unconventional? What's one step you could take this week to lean into it?

Next Chapter Preview:

Chapter 6: Lead with Clarity explores how Apple's relentless focus on simplicity and clarity helped it become the most valuable company in the world—and how you can lead with clarity in your own organization.

6

Lead with
Clarity

The Crisis & The Opportunity

In 1997, Apple was on the brink of bankruptcy. The company had lost its way, producing a confusing array of products that lacked focus and failed to resonate with consumers. Its market share had dwindled to just 3%, and its stock price had plummeted. Many believed Apple was beyond saving. But then, Steve Jobs returned to the company he had co-founded, and everything changed.

Jobs' first order of business was to bring **clarity** to Apple. He slashed the product lineup from over 40 products to just four, focusing on a simple matrix: consumer and professional, desktop and portable. He streamlined operations, cut unnecessary costs, and refocused the company on its core mission: to create beautifully designed, user-friendly products that "just work." This clarity of vision and execution transformed

Apple from a struggling tech company into one of the most valuable and influential brands in the world.

Today, under the leadership of Tim Cook, Apple continues to thrive by maintaining this focus on clarity. From its product design to its marketing campaigns, Apple's commitment to simplicity and clarity has become a hallmark of its success. This chapter explores how Apple's clarity has driven its success—and how you can lead with clarity to achieve extraordinary results in your own organization.

The Story of Apple's Clarity

The Early Days: A Vision for Simplicity

Apple's journey began in 1976, when Steve Jobs and Steve Wozniak co-founded the company in a garage in Cupertino, California. From the beginning, Jobs had a clear vision: to make technology accessible and intuitive for everyone. This vision was embodied in the Apple II, the company's first mass-market computer, which featured a simple, user-friendly design that appealed to both hobbyists and everyday consumers.

But as Apple grew, it lost sight of this clarity. By the 1990s, the company was producing a dizzying array of products, from printers to digital cameras, many of which were poorly designed and failed to resonate with consumers. The lack of focus led to declining sales, internal chaos, and near-bankruptcy.

The Turning Point: Steve Jobs' Return

When Steve Jobs returned to Apple in 1997, he brought with him a relentless focus on clarity. His first step was to simplify Apple's product lineup. He famously drew a 2x2 matrix on a whiteboard, with "Consumer" and "Professional" on one axis and "Desktop" and "Portable" on the other. This matrix became the foundation for Apple's product strategy, resulting in four core products: the iMac, the Power Mac, the iBook, and the PowerBook.

Jobs also brought clarity to Apple's branding and marketing. He partnered with ad agency TBWA\Chiat\Day to create the iconic "Think Different" campaign, which celebrated Apple's mission to challenge the status quo and empower creative thinkers. The campaign was a bold statement of Apple's values and vision, and it resonated deeply with consumers.

The Innovation: Clarity in Design and Functionality

Apple's commitment to clarity is perhaps most evident in its product design. From the iMac to the iPhone, Apple's products are known for their simplicity, elegance, and ease of use. This clarity of design is the result of a relentless focus on the user experience, guided by the principle that technology should "just work."

1. The iMac (1998)

   The iMac was Apple's first major product under Jobs' leadership, and it embodied his vision of clarity. The computer featured a sleek, all-in-one design with a translucent case that made it stand out from the beige boxes of its competitors. But the iMac's real innovation was its simplicity: it was designed to be easy to set up and use, with no complicated manuals or technical jargon.

2. The iPod (2001)

   The iPod revolutionized the music industry with its simple, intuitive interface. Unlike other MP3 players, which were clunky and difficult to use, the iPod featured a scroll wheel that made it easy to navigate thousands of songs. The device's clarity of design and functionality made it a massive success, selling over 400 million units.

3. The iPhone (2007)

   The iPhone was a game-changer, combining a phone, an iPod, and an internet communicator into a single device. Its touchscreen interface was a model of clarity, allowing users to navigate apps and features with just a few taps. The iPhone's success cemented Apple's reputation as a leader in innovation and design.

The Pandemic Test: Clarity in Crisis

When the COVID-19 pandemic hit in 2020, Apple faced new challenges. Supply chains were disrupted, stores were forced to close, and consumer demand was uncertain. But Apple's clarity of vision and execution allowed it to navigate the crisis with remarkable resilience.

Under Tim Cook's leadership, Apple quickly adapted to the new reality. The company shifted to remote work, implemented safety measures in its stores, and accelerated its focus on digital services like Apple Music, Apple TV+, and the App Store. By the end of 2020, Apple had not only weathered the storm but achieved record revenues, surpassing $100 billion in quarterly sales for the first time.

The Human Side: Cultivating a Culture of Clarity

At the heart of Apple's clarity is its culture of focus, discipline, and attention to detail. Employees are encouraged to think deeply, communicate clearly, and strive for excellence in everything they do. This culture is supported by several key practices:

1. Mission-Driven Leadership

   Apple's leaders, from Steve Jobs to Tim Cook, have always been clear about the company's mission: to create products that enrich people's lives. This clarity of purpose inspires employees to work toward a common goal and ensures that everyone is aligned with the company's vision.

2. Simplification

   Apple's culture values simplicity over complexity. Employees are encouraged to strip away unnecessary features and focus on what truly matters. This principle is encapsulated in Jobs' famous quote: "Simplicity is the ultimate sophistication."

3. Attention to Detail

   Apple's products are known for their meticulous attention to detail, from the design of the hardware to the user interface of the software. This focus on detail is a reflection of Apple's culture, which values precision and excellence.

4. Clear Communication

   Apple's leaders are known for their ability to communicate clearly and concisely. Whether it's a product launch or an internal memo, Apple's messaging is always focused, direct, and easy to understand.

The Results: Clarity Fuels Success

By 2023, Apple had become the most valuable company in the world, with a market capitalization exceeding $2.5 trillion. The company's clarity of vision and execution had paid off in several key ways:

- **Product Dominance:** Apple's products, from the iPhone to the MacBook, dominate their respective markets, with loyal customers and high profit margins.

- **Brand Loyalty:** Apple's Net Promoter Score (NPS) is consistently among the highest in the industry, reflecting its deep connection with customers.

- **Financial Performance:** Apple's revenues and profits have grown steadily, driven by its focus on high-margin products and services.

But Apple's real legacy lies in its ability to inspire others. The company's clarity has set a new standard for innovation, design, and customer experience, influencing industries far beyond technology.

Actionable Takeaways for Leaders

1. Define Your Clear Vision

   Clarity starts with a clear, compelling vision that guides your decisions and actions.

   - **Ask:** "What's the one thing we want to be known for?"

   - **Example:** Apple's vision to "create products that enrich people's lives" is both clear and inspiring

   - **Template:** "Our vision is to [achieve a specific outcome] by [focusing on a core mission]."

2. Simplify Your Strategy

   Clarity requires simplicity. Focus on a few key priorities and eliminate distractions.

   - **Conduct a Product Audit:** Review your product or service lineup and eliminate anything that doesn't align with your vision.

   - **Create a Decision Matrix:** Use a simple framework (e.g., Jobs' 2x2 matrix) to prioritize initiatives and allocate resources.

   - **Communicate Clearly:** Use simple, direct language to communicate your strategy to your team and stakeholders.

3. Focus on the User Experience

Clarity in design and functionality is critical to creating products and services that resonate with customers.

- **Observe and Listen:** Spend time with your customers to understand their needs and pain points.

- **Iterate and Refine:** Continuously test and improve your products to ensure they are intuitive and easy to use.

- **Sweat the Details:** Pay attention to every aspect of the user experience, from packaging to customer support.

4. Build a Culture of Clarity

Clarity is not just about strategy—it's about creating a culture that values focus, discipline, and attention to detail.

- **Set Clear Expectations:** Define roles, responsibilities, and goals for your team.

- **Encourage Deep Work:** Create an environment where employees can focus on meaningful, high-impact work.

- **Celebrate Excellence:** Recognize and reward employees who demonstrate clarity and precision in their work.

Pitfalls to Avoid

1. Overcomplicating Your Strategy

   Clarity requires simplicity. Avoid creating overly complex plans or processes.

   - **Fix:** Regularly review your strategy and eliminate unnecessary complexity.

2. Losing Focus

   Clarity is about staying focused on your vision, even in the face of distractions.

   - **Fix:** Regularly revisit your vision and priorities to ensure alignment with your actions.

3. Ignoring Feedback

   Clarity requires a willingness to listen and adapt.

   - **Fix:** Create channels for employees and customers to share feedback and ideas.

Your "Clarity Leadership" Workshop

Step 1: Define Your Clear Vision

- Gather your team and ask: "What's the one thing we want to be known for?"

- Use the **Golden Circle** framework: Start with *Why*, then define *How* and *What*.

Step 2: Simplify Your Strategy

- Conduct a product or service audit to eliminate distractions.

- Create a decision matrix to prioritize initiatives and allocate resources.

Step 3: Focus on the User Experience

- Spend time with your customers to understand their needs and pain points.

- Iterate and refine your products or services to ensure they are intuitive and easy to use.

Step 4: Build a Culture of Clarity

- Set clear expectations for your team and encourage deep work.

- Celebrate excellence and recognize employees who demonstrate clarity and precision.

Chapter Summary

Apple's story proves that clarity is not just a leadership trait—it's a mindset. By defining a clear vision, simplifying your strategy, focusing on the user experience, and building a culture of clarity, you can achieve extraordinary results in your organization. Your next step is to lead with clarity: stay focused, communicate clearly, and create products and services that resonate deeply with your customers.

Think about it: Where is your team drowning in complexity? What's one message or goal you could simplify today to cut through the noise?

Next Chapter Preview:

Chapter 7: Lead with We ('Community') explores how **Chobani** has built a thriving community around its brand by prioritizing inclusivity, social responsibility, and employee empowerment—and how you can lead with a focus on community to drive loyalty and impact in your own organization.

Lead with We ('Community')

The Crisis & The Opportunity

In 2005, Hamdi Ulukaya, a Turkish immigrant living in upstate New York, purchased a shuttered yogurt factory with a small business loan. His vision was simple: to bring the rich, creamy yogurt of his homeland to the American market. What started as a modest operation quickly grew into **Chobani**, one of the most successful food brands in the U.S. By 2023, Chobani had become the #1 selling Greek yogurt brand in America, with annual revenues exceeding $2 billion.

But Chobani's success isn't just about yogurt. It's about community. From its early days, Chobani has been driven by a mission to make better food for more people, while also making a positive impact on the world. The company has built a loyal following by prioritizing inclusivity, social responsibility, and employee empowerment. This chapter explores how Chobani's community-driven approach has fueled its success—and how you can lead with a focus on community to drive loyalty and impact in your own organization.

The Story of Chobani's Community

The Early Days: A Mission to Make Better Food

Chobani's story begins with Hamdi Ulukaya, who grew up in a small village in Turkey, where yogurt was a staple of the diet. When he moved to the U.S., he was disappointed by the lack of high-quality, authentic yogurt available in stores. In 2005, he saw an opportunity to change that when he came across a shuttered yogurt factory in South Edmeston, New York. With a small business loan and a handful of employees, Ulukaya set out to create a yogurt that was both delicious and nutritious.

From the beginning, Ulukaya's mission was clear: to make better food for more people. This mission wasn't just about taste—it was about accessibility. Ulukaya wanted to create a product that was affordable and available to everyone, not just a niche market. This focus on inclusivity became a cornerstone of Chobani's brand and culture.

The Turning Point: The Rise of Greek Yogurt

When Chobani launched in 2007, Greek yogurt was virtually unknown in the U.S. market. But Ulukaya believed in the product's potential. He focused on creating a yogurt that was thick, creamy, and packed with protein, unlike the thin, sugary yogurts that dominated store shelves. He also made a bold decision to sell Chobani in larger, single-serve cups, which were more convenient for consumers.

The gamble paid off. By 2012, Chobani had become the #1 selling Greek yogurt brand in America, with annual revenues exceeding $1 billion. The company's success was driven by its commitment to quality, its innovative packaging, and its ability to connect with consumers on a deeper level.

The Innovation: Building a Community-Driven Brand

Chobani's success isn't just about its product—it's about its ability to build a community around its brand. The company has done this in several key ways:

1. Inclusivity and Accessibility

    Chobani's mission to make better food for more people is reflected in its pricing and distribution. The company has worked to keep its products affordable and widely available, even as it has expanded into new markets. This focus on inclusivity has helped Chobani build a loyal customer base that spans all demographics.

2. Social Responsibility

   Chobani has always been committed to making a positive impact on the world. The company donates 10% of its profits to charitable causes, including hunger relief, refugee support, and environmental sustainability. Chobani also launched the **Chobani Incubator**, a program that supports food startups focused on health and wellness.

3. Employee Empowerment

   Chobani's employees, whom the company calls "Chobaniacs," are at the heart of its success. The company offers competitive wages, benefits, and opportunities for advancement, and it has a strong focus on diversity and inclusion. In 2016, Ulukaya made headlines when he gave 10% of the company's equity to his employees, a bold move that underscored his commitment to sharing Chobani's success with those who helped build it.

The Pandemic Test: Community in Crisis

When the COVID-19 pandemic hit in 2020, Chobani's commitment to community was put to the test. The company faced unprecedented challenges, including supply chain disruptions, workforce shortages, and surging demand for its products. But Chobani responded with bold, decisive actions that reinforced its community-driven values.

Chobani donated millions of dollars' worth of yogurt and other products to food banks and frontline workers. The company also implemented safety measures to protect its employees, including enhanced cleaning protocols, PPE, and paid sick leave. Despite the challenges, Chobani's sales grew by 10% in 2020, a testament to the strength of its brand and its connection with consumers.

The Human Side: Cultivating a Culture of Community

At the heart of Chobani's success is its culture of inclusivity, empowerment, and social responsibility. Employees are encouraged to take ownership of their work, collaborate across teams, and contribute to the company's mission. This culture is supported by several key practices:

1. Mission-Driven Leadership

    Hamdi Ulukaya's vision for Chobani is not just about making yogurt—it's about making a positive impact on the world. This mission inspires employees to work toward a larger purpose, giving them a sense of pride and fulfillment in their work.

2. Diversity and Inclusion

   Chobani's workforce is one of the most diverse in the food industry, with employees from over 20 countries. The company has a strong focus on creating an inclusive environment where everyone feels valued and respected.

3. Employee Ownership

   Chobani's decision to give 10% of its equity to employees was a bold statement of its commitment to sharing success. This move not only rewarded employees for their hard work but also aligned their interests with the company's long-term goals.

4. Community Engagement

   Chobani's employees are encouraged to get involved in their communities, whether through volunteering, charitable giving, or participating in company-sponsored initiatives. This focus on community engagement fosters a sense of connection and purpose among employees.

The Results: Community Fuels Success

By 2023, Chobani had solidified its position as the #1 selling Greek yogurt brand in America, with a market share of over 40%. The company's community-driven approach had paid off in several key ways:

- **Customer Loyalty:** Chobani's Net Promoter Score (NPS) is consistently among the highest in the food industry, reflecting its deep connection with customers.

- **Employee Satisfaction:** Chobani's employee turnover rate is significantly lower than the industry average, thanks to its inclusive culture and focus on empowerment.

- **Social Impact:** Chobani's charitable initiatives and community programs have made a tangible difference in the lives of millions of people.

But Chobani's real legacy lies in its ability to inspire others. The company's community-driven approach has shown that a brand can thrive by prioritizing people, purpose, and impact.

Actionable Takeaways for Leaders

1. Define Your Community Mission

   Community starts with a clear, compelling mission that guides your decisions and actions.

   - **Ask:** "What's the positive impact we want to make in our community or industry?"

   - **Example:** Chobani's mission to "make better food for more people" is both clear and inclusive.

- **Template:** "Our mission is to [achieve a specific outcome] by [focusing on a core mission]."

2. Prioritize Inclusivity and Accessibility

   Community-driven brands prioritize inclusivity, ensuring that their products and services are accessible to all.

   - **Offer Affordable Options:** Keep your products or services affordable and widely available.

   - **Focus on Diversity:** Create an inclusive environment where everyone feels valued and respected.

   - **Engage All Stakeholders:** Build relationships with customers, employees, and community partners.

3. Invest in Social Responsibility

   Community-driven brands are committed to making a positive impact on the world.

   - **Donate a Percentage of Profits:** Commit to giving back to charitable causes.

- **Support Local Communities:** Partner with local organizations to address community needs.

- **Launch Impact Initiatives:** Create programs that align with your mission and values.

4. Empower Your Employees

   Your employees are the heart of your community. Empower them to take ownership of their work and contribute to your mission.

   - **Share Success:** Consider equity-sharing or profit-sharing programs to reward employees.

   - **Encourage Collaboration:** Foster a culture of teamwork and cross-functional collaboration.

   - **Provide Growth Opportunities:** Invest in training and development to help employees grow.

Pitfalls to Avoid

1. Tokenism

   Community-driven initiatives must be genuine and impactful, not just for show.

   - **Fix:** Ensure that your actions align with your mission and values.

2. Ignoring Feedback

   Community-driven brands must be open to feedback and willing to adapt.

   - **Fix:** Create channels for employees and customers to share feedback and ideas.

3. Overextending Resources

   Community initiatives require resources, but overextending can lead to burnout and failure.

   - **Fix:** Prioritize initiatives and allocate resources strategically.

Your "Community Leadership" Workshop

Step 1: Define Your Community Mission

   - Gather your team and ask: "What's the positive impact we want to make in our community or industry?"

   - Use the **Golden Circle** framework: Start with *Why*, then define *How* and *What*.

Step 2: Identify Community Opportunities

   - Brainstorm initiatives that align with your mission and values.

- Use the **Impact Mapping** framework: "What actions can we take to make a tangible difference?"

Step 3: Create a Community Action Plan

- Identify 2–3 community initiatives to pursue in the next 90 days.

- Assign ownership and resources to each initiative.

- Set milestones to track progress and celebrate successes.

Chapter Summary

Chobani's story proves that community is not just a buzzword—it's a powerful driver of success. By defining a clear mission, prioritizing inclusivity, investing in social responsibility, and empowering employees, Chobani has built a brand that resonates deeply with customers and makes a positive impact on the world. Your next step is to lead with community: prioritize people, purpose, and impact, and create a culture where everyone feels connected and valued.

Think about it: Who in your ecosystem (employees, customers, partners) feels excluded? What's one action you could take to bridge that gap?

Next Chapter Preview:

Chapter 8: Lead with Compassion explores how leaders like Satya Nadella (Microsoft), Hamdi Ulukaya (Chobani), and Yvon Chouinard (Patagonia) have redefined leadership by prioritizing empathy, well-being, and community. Discover how compassion became a cornerstone of modern leadership during the pandemic—and how you can lead with compassion to build trust, foster resilience, and create lasting impact in your organization and beyond.

Lead with Compassion

The Crisis & The Opportunity

In 2020, as the COVID-19 pandemic swept across the globe, leaders were faced with an unprecedented challenge: how to navigate a crisis that affected every aspect of life—health, work, family, and community. Amid the chaos, one leadership quality emerged as a defining factor for success: **compassion**. Leaders who prioritized empathy, understanding, and care for their employees, customers, and communities not only survived the crisis but thrived. They built trust, loyalty, and resilience in ways that will have a lasting impact for years to come.

Compassion is often seen as a "soft" skill, something nice to have but not essential for leadership. But the events of the past few years have proven otherwise. Compassion is not just a moral imperative—it's a strategic advantage. In a world where uncertainty and disruption are the new normal, leaders who lead with compassion are the ones who inspire, unite, and create lasting change.

This chapter explores how compassion has become a cornerstone of modern leadership, and how you can lead with compassion to build trust, foster resilience, and drive meaningful impact in your organization and beyond.

The Story of Compassionate Leadership

The Early Days: A Shift in Leadership Paradigms

For decades, leadership was often associated with traits like decisiveness, authority, and control. The image of the "strong leader" who made tough decisions without hesitation was held up as the ideal. But as the world became more complex and interconnected, this model began to show its limitations. Employees, customers, and communities started demanding more from their leaders—not just competence, but care.

The shift toward compassionate leadership began to gain traction in the early 2000s, as companies like Google and Zappos started prioritizing employee well-being and psychological safety. But it wasn't until the pandemic that compassion became a non-negotiable for leaders everywhere. Overnight, leaders were forced to confront the human side of their organizations—the fears, struggles, and vulnerabilities of their employees and customers. And those who responded with compassion reaped the rewards.

The Turning Point: The Pandemic as a Catalyst for Compassion

When the pandemic hit in 2020, leaders were faced with a choice: prioritize profits or prioritize people. Companies that chose the latter—like **Patagonia**, **Microsoft**, and **Chobani**—emerged stronger, with deeper trust and loyalty from their employees and customers.

Patagonia, for example, closed its stores and offices early in the pandemic, prioritizing the safety of its employees and customers. The company also continued to pay its workers, even when stores were closed, and offered mental health resources to help them cope with the crisis. This compassionate approach not only strengthened Patagonia's brand but also reinforced its mission to "save our home planet."

Similarly, Microsoft under Satya Nadella's leadership prioritized employee well-being, offering flexible work arrangements, mental health resources, and paid time off for caregivers. Nadella's emphasis on empathy and compassion became a defining feature of Microsoft's culture, earning the company widespread praise and loyalty.

The Innovation: Compassion as a Competitive Advantage

Compassionate leadership is not just about being kind—it's about creating a culture where people feel valued, supported, and empowered to do their best work. Companies that have embraced this approach have seen tangible benefits, from higher employee engagement to stronger customer loyalty.

1. Employee Well-Being

   Compassionate leaders prioritize the physical, mental, and emotional well-being of their employees. This includes offering flexible work arrangements, mental health resources, and opportunities for growth and development. Companies like **Salesforce** and **Google** have set the standard for employee well-being, with programs like wellness stipends, mindfulness training, and paid sabbaticals.

2. Psychological Safety

   Compassionate leaders create an environment where employees feel safe to speak up, take risks, and make mistakes. This concept, known as psychological safety, is a key driver of innovation and collaboration. Companies like **Netflix** and **Spotify** have embraced psychological safety by encouraging open dialogue, radical candor, and a culture of learning from failure.

3. Community Engagement

   Compassionate leaders understand that their responsibility extends beyond their organization to the communities they serve. This includes supporting local initiatives, addressing social and environmental issues, and giving back in meaningful ways. Companies like **Chobani** and **Patagonia** have made community engagement a core part of their mission, earning them deep trust and loyalty from their customers.

The Pandemic Test: Compassion in Action

The pandemic was a litmus test for compassionate leadership. Companies that prioritized compassion not only survived the crisis but emerged stronger, with deeper trust and loyalty from their employees and customers. Here are a few examples:

- **Microsoft:** Under Satya Nadella's leadership, Microsoft prioritized employee well-being, offering flexible work arrangements, mental health resources, and paid time off for caregivers. The company also donated millions of dollars to support pandemic relief efforts.

- **Chobani:** Chobani donated millions of dollars' worth of yogurt and other products to food banks and frontline workers. The company also implemented safety measures to protect its employees, including enhanced cleaning protocols, PPE, and paid sick leave.

- **Patagonia:** Patagonia closed its stores and offices early in the pandemic, prioritizing the safety of its employees and customers. The company also continued to pay its workers, even when stores were closed, and offered mental health resources to help them cope with the crisis.

The Human Side: Cultivating a Culture of Compassion

At the heart of compassionate leadership is a culture of empathy, understanding, and care. This culture is supported by several key practices:

1. Empathy

   Compassionate leaders are deeply empathetic. They take the time to understand the needs, fears, and aspirations of their employees and customers. This empathy allows them to make decisions that are not just good for the business, but good for people.

2. Vulnerability

   Compassionate leaders are not afraid to show their vulnerability. They admit their mistakes, share their struggles, and ask for help when they need it. This vulnerability creates a culture of trust and openness, where employees feel safe to do the same.

3. Support

   Compassionate leaders prioritize the well-being of their employees. This includes offering flexible work arrangements, mental health resources, and opportunities for growth and development. It also means creating a culture where employees feel supported and valued.

4. Community

   Compassionate leaders understand that their responsibility extends beyond their organization to the communities they serve. This includes supporting local initiatives, addressing social and environmental issues, and giving back in meaningful ways.

The Results: Compassion Fuels Success

By 2023, companies that embraced compassionate leadership had seen tangible benefits, from higher employee engagement to stronger customer loyalty. Here are a few examples:

- **Employee Engagement:** Companies that prioritize employee well-being and psychological safety have higher levels of employee engagement and lower turnover rates. For example, Google's employee engagement scores are consistently among the highest in the tech industry.

- **Customer Loyalty:** Companies that prioritize community engagement and social responsibility have stronger customer loyalty. For example, Patagonia's Net Promoter Score (NPS) is consistently among the highest in the retail industry.

- **Innovation:** Companies that create a culture of psychological safety and open dialogue are more innovative. For example, Netflix's culture of radical candor has fueled its ability to innovate and stay ahead of the competition.

But the real legacy of compassionate leadership lies in its ability to create lasting impact. Companies that lead with compassion don't just build successful businesses—they build a better world.

Actionable Takeaways for Leaders

1. Practice Empathy

   Compassionate leadership starts with empathy. Take the time to understand the needs, fears, and aspirations of your employees and customers.

   - **Listen Actively:** Practice active listening by giving your full attention to the person speaking and reflecting back what you hear.

   - **Ask Open-Ended Questions:** Use open-ended questions to encourage dialogue and understanding.

   - **Show Genuine Care:** Demonstrate your care through your words and actions.

2. Embrace Vulnerability

   Compassionate leaders are not afraid to show their vulnerability. Admit your mistakes, share your struggles, and ask for help when you need it.

   - **Share Your Story:** Share your own experiences with failure and growth to create a culture of openness.

- **Admit Mistakes:** When you make a mistake, admit it openly and take responsibility.

- **Ask for Feedback:** Regularly ask for feedback from your team and be open to constructive criticism.

3. Prioritize Well-Being

Compassionate leaders prioritize the physical, mental, and emotional well-being of their employees.

- **Offer Flexibility:** Provide flexible work arrangements to support work-life balance.

- **Provide Resources:** Offer mental health resources, wellness programs, and opportunities for growth.

- **Create a Supportive Culture:** Foster a culture where employees feel supported and valued.

4. Engage with Your Community

Compassionate leaders understand that their responsibility extends beyond their organization to the communities they serve.

- **Support Local Initiatives:** Partner with local organizations to address community needs.

- **Address Social Issues:** Take a stand on social and environmental issues that align with your mission.

- **Give Back:** Donate time, resources, and expertise to support meaningful causes.

Pitfalls to Avoid

1. Tokenism

   Compassionate leadership must be genuine and impactful, not just for show.

   - **Fix:** Ensure that your actions align with your mission and values.

2. Ignoring Feedback

   Compassionate leaders must be open to feedback and willing to adapt.

   - **Fix:** Create channels for employees and customers to share feedback and ideas.

3. Overextending Resources

   Compassionate initiatives require resources, but overextending can lead to burnout and failure.

   - **Fix:** Prioritize initiatives and allocate resources strategically.

Your "Compassionate Leadership" Workshop

Step 1: Practice Empathy

- Gather your team and ask: "What's one thing you're struggling with right now?"

- Use active listening techniques to understand and reflect back what you hear.

Step 2: Embrace Vulnerability

- Share a personal story of failure or growth with your team.

- Ask for feedback on how you can better support them.

Step 3: Prioritize Well-Being

- Identify one initiative to support employee well-being (e.g., wellness stipends, mental health resources).

- Create a plan to implement the initiative within the next 90 days.

Step 4: Engage with Your Community

- Identify one community initiative to support (e.g., local food bank, environmental organization).

- Create a plan to engage your team in the initiative (e.g., volunteer day, donation drive).

Chapter Summary

Compassionate leadership is not just a moral imperative—it's a strategic advantage. By practicing empathy, embracing vulnerability, prioritizing well-being, and engaging with your community, you can build trust, foster resilience, and drive meaningful impact in your organization and beyond. Your next step is to lead with compassion: show up, be present, and care deeply for the people you serve.

Think about it: When was the last time you asked your team, "How are you really doing?" How can you make compassion a daily ritual, not a crisis response?

Next Chapter Preview:

Bonus Chapter: The Path Forward – Leading in the Now of Work and Beyond brings everything together, guiding you on how to actualize the principles of purpose, authenticity, adaptability, boldness, clarity, community, and compassion in your leadership journey. As you step into the future, this chapter will inspire you to create a legacy that matters, offering a step-by-step roadmap to transform your leadership and make a lasting impact on the world.

PART III

The Path Forward

The Path Forward – Leading in The Now of Work and Beyond

Your Zen Leadership Journey in a World of Uncertainty

A Letter to the Reader

Dear friend and ally,

As you stand at the threshold of today and tomorrow, the world around you is a tapestry of complexity. Polarization, economic volatility, and cultural shifts test leaders daily. Institutions are strained, trust is fragile, and the pace of change feels unrelenting. Yet in this turbulence lies opportunity—not just to survive, but to lead with intention, integrity, and impact.

This chapter is not about external forces or political figures. It's about *you*. How will *you* navigate this landscape? How will *you* turn challenges into catalysts for growth? The Zen Leadership habits we've explored—**purpose, authenticity, adaptability, boldness, clarity, community, and compassion**—are your tools to forge a path that matters. Let's begin.

The World As It Is: Your Leadership Crucible

The socio-political and economic landscape is marked by:

- **Deepening Polarization:** Public discourse is fractured, with trust in media, government, and even science eroded by misinformation and ideological divides.

- **Economic Volatility:** Supply chain disruptions, inflation, and climate-driven market shifts demand agility and resilience.

- **Cultural Reckonings:** Debates over equity, identity, and sustainability reveal both progress and backlash.

But these are not obstacles—they are invitations. Invitations to lead differently.

Your Zen Leadership Framework: Revisited

Let's reconnect the habits to *your* journey:

1. Lead with Purpose

Why It Matters Now: In a noisy world, purpose is your compass. It cuts through chaos and aligns your team around what's enduring.

- *Your Move:* Conduct a "Purpose Audit." Ask:

    ○ "Does our mission still resonate in today's world?"

    ○ "Where are we reacting to noise instead of leading with intent?"

- *Example:* When outdoor retailer REI closed on Black Friday to advocate for nature over consumerism, it reaffirmed its purpose—and galvanized loyal customers.

2. Lead with Authenticity

Why It Matters Now: Trust is scarce. Authenticity rebuilds it.

- *Your Move:* Practice radical transparency. Share your struggles, failures, and lessons openly.

- *Example:* Airbnb's CEO Brian Chesky's candid layoff emails during COVID-19 ("I'm truly sorry") humanized leadership and deepened employee trust.

3. Lead with Adaptability

Why It Matters Now: Change is the only constant. Agility is survival.

- *Your Move:* Run "Adaptability Sprints." For example:

  ○ Pilot a hybrid work model in one team for 30 days. Learn. Iterate. Scale.

- *Example:* Spotify's "Squad Model" let teams pivot swiftly during the pandemic, accelerating podcast dominance.

4. Lead with Boldness

Why It Matters Now: Safe choices rarely make history.

- *Your Move:* Identify one "moonshot" idea that aligns with your purpose. Prototype it in 90 days.

- *Example:* Chobani's decision to hire refugees in its factories was bold, controversial, and ultimately transformative for its brand and culture.

5. Lead with Clarity

Why It Matters Now: Misinformation and overload paralyze teams. Clarity empowers action.

- *Your Move:* Simplify. Use the "One-Page Strategy": Distill goals, priorities, and metrics onto a single page.

- *Example:* Apple's product launches focus on 1–2 game-changing features, cutting through tech clutter.

6. Lead with Community

Why It Matters Now: Loneliness and division are rampant. Community heals.

- *Your Move:* Build "micro-communities" at work. Example: Peer mentorship circles, wellness groups, or innovation pods.

- *Example:* HEB's localized disaster response during Texas' 2021 freeze turned stores into community hubs, saving lives and loyalty.

7. Lead with Compassion

Why It Matters Now: Burnout and anxiety are endemic. Compassion fuels resilience.

- *Your Move:* Implement "Compassion Rituals":

  ○ Start meetings with a mindfulness minute.

  ○ Normalize "no-camera Fridays" to reduce Zoom fatigue.

- *Example:* Microsoft's company-wide mental health days and LinkedIn's skills-first hiring prioritize well-being over hustle.

Your Action Plan: Building a Timeless Legacy

Step 1: Start with Self

- *Reflect:* Journal on these questions:
  - "What legacy do I want to leave?"
  - "Which Zen habit feels most urgent for me to strengthen?"
- *Act:* Commit to one daily ritual (e.g., 5 minutes of mindfulness, a gratitude practice) to ground your leadership.

Step 2: Empower Your Team

- *Diagnose:* Survey your team anonymously:
  - "Do you feel safe to take risks here?"
  - "What's one change that would improve your well-being?"
- *Prototype:* Test a "Flexible Friday" with no meetings, only deep work or creative projects.

Step 3: Engage Your Ecosystem

- *Map Stakeholders:* Identify key partners, customers, and communities. Ask:

    o "How can we support their needs now?"

    o "Where can we collaborate instead of compete?"

- *Launch a "Bridge-Building" Initiative:* Partner with a local nonprofit or school to address a shared challenge (e.g., digital literacy, food insecurity).

Think about it: If you were to write your leadership legacy today, what would it say? What's one habit you'll commit to starting tomorrow to make it real?

The Ripple Effect: Your Leadership Legacy

Leadership is not about control—it's about influence. Every decision you make, every interaction you have, sends ripples into the world. In the now and beyond of work, your Zen Leadership habits will determine whether those ripples spread division or healing, fear or hope.

Final Thought:

The world doesn't need more critics. It needs more builders—leaders like *you* who choose courage over cynicism, compassion over judgment, and purpose over noise. The road ahead is yours to shape.

With unwavering belief in your journey,

Tim Salau,
Mr. FoW

P.S. It might be a while until you get another book like this from me...

Index

Z

- Zen Leadership habits
  - Worksheets

Appendices

Appendix A: Zen Leadership Worksheets

Tools to Turn Insight into Action

1. Purpose Audit Worksheet

   o *Step 1:* Define your organization's mission.

   o *Step 2:* List current policies/practices.

   o *Step 3:* Identify misalignments.

   o *Step 4:* Draft a realignment plan.

2. Adaptability Sprint Planner

   o *Template:* 30-day experiment framework (Goal, Team, Metrics, Reflection).

3. One-Page Strategy Builder

   o *Sections:* Core mission, 3 priorities, success metrics, stakeholder impact.

4. Compassion Ritual Calendar

   o *Examples:* "Mindfulness Mondays," "No-Camera Fridays," quarterly wellness check-ins.

5. Legacy Journal Prompts

   ○ Questions:

     ■ "What do I want my leadership to be remembered for?"

     ■ "What's one habit I need to amplify to leave this legacy?"

     ■ "What's one bold decision I've been avoiding, and how could taking that step align with the legacy I want to leave?"

Appendix B: Further Reading & Resources

Curated Wisdom for Zen Leaders

Books

1. Start With Why: How Great Leaders Inspire Everyone to Take Action by Simon Sinek

   - *Why It's Relevant:* Explores the power of purpose and how leaders can inspire action by starting with "Why."

2. Dare to Lead: Brave Work. Tough Conversations. Whole Hearts. by Brené Brown

   - *Why It's Relevant:* Focuses on vulnerability, courage, and trust as pillars of accountable and empathetic leadership.

3. We Should All Be Millionaires: A Woman's Guide to Earning More, Building Wealth, and Gaining Economic Power by Rachel Rodgers

   - *Why It's Relevant:* Empowers leaders—especially women—to embrace boldness, challenge systemic barriers, and build financial independence.

Articles & Reports

1. "Leadership Accountability: What It Looks Like, Why It Matters" (The Washington Post)

   ○ *Why It's Relevant:* Examines how accountability shapes company culture and performance.

2. "Leadership Accountability: How to Build It Into Your Culture" (Betterworks)

   ○ *Why It's Relevant:* Offers strategies for embedding accountability into organizational culture.

3. "The Power of Accountability in Leadership" (LinkedIn)

   ○ *Why It's Relevant:* Explores how accountability empowers leaders to build high-performing teams.

Podcasts & TED Talks

1. Simon Sinek: "How Great Leaders Inspire Action" (TED)

   ○ *Why It's Relevant:* Highlights the role of purpose in fostering accountability and inspiring teams.

2. Brené Brown: "The Power of Vulnerability" (TED)

- ○ *Why It's Relevant:* Explores how vulnerability builds trust and accountability in leadership.

3. "The Look & Sound of Leadership" (Podcast by Tom Henschel)

- ○ *Why It's Relevant:* Focuses on effective communication and accountability in leadership.

Documentaries

1. The Social Dilemma (Netflix)

- ○ *Why It's Relevant:* Examines the ethical responsibilities of leaders in the tech industry.

2. Inside Bill's Brain: Decoding Bill Gates (Netflix)

- ○ *Why It's Relevant:* Showcases how accountability and problem-solving drive impactful leadership.

Appendix C: About the Author

Tim Salau – Mr. Future of Work

Tim Salau is a visionary strategist, keynote speaker, and CEO of Guide, a mental health platform redefining wellness and leadership for the modern workforce. Dubbed "Mr. Future of Work" by Forbes, Tim has advised Fortune 500 companies, startups, and governments on building resilient, human-centric organizations.

A first-generation Nigerian-American, Tim's mission is rooted in equity and accessibility. He's spoken at TEDx, SXSW, and the United Nations, advocating for workplaces where purpose and profit coexist.

When not writing or speaking, Tim mentors underrepresented entrepreneurs and plays NBA 2k25 to "unplug and reconnect with the bigger picture."

Connect with Tim:

- Website: www.timsalau.com

- LinkedIn: Tim Salau

- Twitter: @mrfow777

Appendix D: Zen Leadership Model Diagram

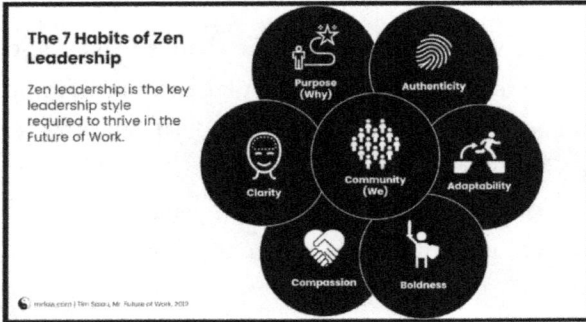

The 7 Habits of Zen Leadership

Zen leadership is the key leadership style required to thrive in the Future of Work.

Purpose (Why)
Authenticity
Clarity
Community (We)
Adaptability
Compassion
Boldness